CLICK!

FUN WITH PHOTOGRAPHY

Susanna Price & Tim Stephens

Belitha Press

First published in Great Britain in 1995 by

Belitha Press Limited
London House
Great Eastern Wharf
Parkgate Road
London SW11 4NQ

ISBN 1-85561-159-7

Printed in China for Imago

British Library Cataloguing in Publication Data for this book is
available from the British Library

Photography by: Susanna Price
Editor: Ann Kay
Designer: Helen James

Talbot Fox illustrations
and dinosaur model: Guy Callaby
Other illustrations (23, 33, 37): Helen James

The publishers would like to thank the following
for their invaluable help with this book:
Archway Pool, north London; British Waterways;
the Joyce, MacDonald, Marriot-Dixson, Pick and
Schaffer families; Hackney City Farm, north
London; Mosquito Bikes (UK) Ltd, London; Nikon
UK Ltd, London; Techno Retail Ltd, Euston Road,
London; the staff, pupils and parents at William
Tyndale School, north London.

Words in **bold** appear in the glossary on page 44.

Contents

Introduction

Everyone can take great photographs with the huge range of light, easy-to-use cameras around today. We see photos around us wherever we go, in magazines and newspapers and in advertisements in the street. But most of the photos taken today are shots of family, friends, school and holidays snapped by ordinary people.

These photos can be just as powerful and exciting as a professional photographer's and they are great fun to take. You don't need lots of equipment, just plenty of enthusiasm and ideas and a basic camera.

CHECKLIST

✔ From time to time, you will see a checklist that looks like this

✔ The checklist sums up the main points made in the text near the checklist

✔ When you have finished the book, you can use the checklists as handy reminders of some of the basic principles

Click! Fun with Photography takes you a step at a time through the basics of photography, from choosing a camera to making the most of your flash. There are also plenty of ideas for projects which will make the most of your skills and equipment.

The book concentrates on taking photos with a fairly simple compact camera. There is also extra information on how to use a more complex compact or a single lens reflex (SLR) camera.

Most of the information on SLRs is in the Talbot's Tips boxes. These are introduced by Talbot Fox (below), who is named after one of the early pioneers of photography – an Englishman called Fox Talbot who lived in the 1800s. Talbot Fox explains more complex techniques.

CLICK START

There are all kinds of good cameras available, in a huge variety of prices. Choices range from disposable cameras that are thrown away when the film is processed, through easy-to-use compacts, to more complex models called single lens reflex (SLR) cameras.

CHOOSING A CAMERA

When choosing a camera you need to think about which type will suit you best, as well as how much money you have to spend.

● Disposable cameras are very simple, fixed-focus cameras which you simply point and shoot. They work well if there is enough light.

● Compact cameras guarantee good photos in most conditions because their controls adjust automatically.

● Advanced compact cameras have manual controls, which you can alter yourself.

● Single lens reflex cameras give you even more control over the photos you are taking.

● There are also cameras designed for special conditions, such as taking photos underwater.

▲ DISPOSABLE

These **automatic** cameras look like large boxes of **film**. The film is built into the camera case. When you have finished your film, you hand the camera to a film-processor, who pulls apart the case to develop the film. The camera can't be used again.

▲ BASIC COMPACT

Simple compact cameras have a **viewfinder** which has markers that help you frame your picture. They have a **lens** that can cope with most ordinary conditions. They also have automatic focus, **exposure** and **flash** (which can often be turned off). Many compacts automatically detect the speed of film you put in them.

6

0

6

◄ ADVANCED COMPACT

Advanced compact cameras often load, wind on and rewind film automatically. They may have a lens which lets you zoom in close or take wide-angle shots. Many have a display panel that tells you what is happening and some models can even cut down **camera shake**.

►SPECIAL CAMERAS

There are also cameras that can do special things. This model is a waterproof underwater camera. As you can make few adjustments underwater, it has automatic focus and exposure and built-in flash.

▲ SINGLE LENS REFLEX

When you use an SLR camera, the image you see through the viewfinder is exactly what the lens sees. The two are not quite the same on a compact camera, which can cause problems with close-ups. Many SLRs have both manual and automatic controls. When you want to use flash, you need to fix a **flash unit** to the top of the camera.

CHECKLIST

✓ Choose the right camera for the photos you want to take

✓ Disposable cameras are ideal for taking simple photos in good light

✓ Compacts are fine for taking photos in most conditions

✓ In difficult conditions you may need an SLR camera

7

HOW A CAMERA WORKS

Every camera works in the same basic way. The positions of the main features that you find on all modern cameras are marked on the compact camera below. The numbered key explains how they work. A few other common features of cameras are also shown.

● When you take a photograph light travels through the lens of the camera and on to the film inside.

● The diagram on the right shows how the image forms upside down on the film because of the way rays of light enter the lens.

● If film was exposed to light all the time it would become **fogged** (clouded). To stop this, a camera has a **shutter** rather like a door.

● When you press the button on your camera, the shutter opens, letting in light.

FRONT VIEW

1 Shutter release button
This opens the shutter to let in light. The amount of light depends on how long the shutter stays open – the shutter speed. It also depends on the size of a hole inside the camera called the **aperture**. The shutter speed and the aperture control the amount of light going through. This is known as the exposure. Both can be changed manually or automatically.

2 Viewfinder
Looking through this window shows you roughly what will appear in your photograph.

3 Lens
Camera lenses are made of glass or plastic. They bend light rays to form an image on the film. Moving the lens closer to or further from the film focuses the image (makes it look sharp).

4 Auto-focus window
A light beam comes out of the auto-focus window and measures how far away the subject is from the camera.

5 Flash unit
This gives an extra flash of light when light levels are low.

6 Flash-on button
Turns on the flash.

TAKING A PHOTO

This diagram shows how a camera lens focuses on your subject and an image is formed on the film inside the camera.

● Light rays reflected from the subject pass through the lens.

● The shutter lets through these rays and they also pass through the aperture (shutter and aperture are the same thing on some cameras).

● Passing through the curved lens makes the rays bend in and cross. Because they cross, the image formed on the film is upside down.

● How much the light is bent controls the **focusing**.

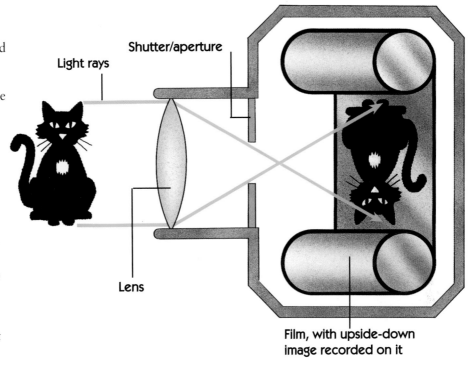

Light rays

Shutter/aperture

Lens

Film, with upside-down image recorded on it

BACK VIEW

7 Film take-up spool
As you use up a film, it is wound around this spool.

8 Film chamber
This is where you put the film cassette when loading the camera.

9 Flash ready light
This light tells you when the flash is ready to go off.

TALBOT'S TIPS

Here is some more information about lenses on SLR cameras, or compacts with manual controls.

● You can buy a range of lenses for all SLRs, and some compacts have an adjustable **zoom lens**. Different lenses have different **focal lengths**. The focal length is the light-bending power of a lens. A short focal length means that you will get a wider angle of view. Focal length is measured in millimetres, and the focal length of a standard SLR lens is about 50mm.

● The shorter the lens the greater the **depth of field**. The depth of field is the area in front of and behind the subject you have focused on, that is also in focus.

◄ This zoom lens is like several different lenses in one. You can adjust its focal length to give a range of views from wide angle to close-up. At the right-hand end of the lens are markings called **f-stops**. Changing the f-stop alters the size of the aperture.

► This photo was taken with a **macro lens**. These lenses are designed for close-up work, as most **standard lenses** don't focus well on subjects which are closer than one metre away.

◄ Standard lenses give a reasonably wide view and fairly large depth of field – although our eyes can see a much wider view than this.

► A **wide-angle lens** fits a much wider view into the picture. These lenses range from 18mm to 35mm. An 18mm lens is called a **fish-eye lens**. It fits so much in that the image curves inwards at the edges.

CHOOSING FILM

All photographic film works in the same way. It is coated with a substance that is sensitive to light.

● When the film is exposed to light, an image is formed on the film. The film is then removed from the camera and processed. **Prints** or **slides** are produced from this processed film.

● The three main types of film are shown below. The different **film speeds** are given **ISO** (International Standards Organization) numbers.

● For poor lighting conditions and fast-moving subjects, use a fast film such as ISO 400.

● In bright light or when using flash, work with slower films such as ISO 100 or 200.

Most film comes in cassettes like this

BLACK AND WHITE FILM

In the early days of photography, only black and white film was available. Most people now use colour film and black and white prints are quite expensive. But you can achieve stunning results with black and white.

This pattern – the **DX code** – tells some kinds of camera the speed of the film

COLOUR SLIDE FILM

This gives a **positive image** (right) when processed, and is made into slides. The other two films on this page produce **negative** images (where light areas are dark and dark areas are light), from which prints are made.

Colour negative

COLOUR PRINT FILM

Colour print film is the most popular type. When the film is processed, you get a negative (see left) and from this prints are produced. All colour films are made from three light-sensitive layers sandwiched together. Between them, these layers record all the different colours in the **light spectrum**.

LOADING FILM

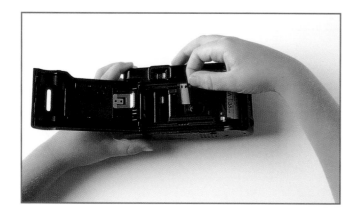

1 Place the camera face down on a flat, clean surface, away from bright light, and open the back. Put the film in the film chamber on the right. Carefully start to pull out the film leader towards the left.

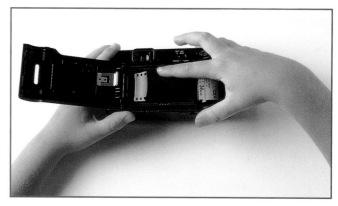

2 Position the film so that it fits over the teeth (if there are any) on the take-up spool. Make sure that you only pull out enough film to line up with the position marked on your camera.

3 Before you close the camera back, check that the film is flat and resting properly between the film guides. Make sure that the back of the camera is firmly closed.

4 On many compacts, if you press the shutter release button down half-way, the film automatically winds on so that it is ready for the first picture to be taken. You will then see the film counter set at number 1.

TALBOT'S TIPS

● Some compacts, and all SLRs, need more manual loading. On SLRs, pull out just enough film to reach the take-up spool. Put the film leader into the slot in the spool (if there is a slot). By alternately using the wind-on lever and pressing the shutter button, wind the film on to the spool until all the leader is taken up. Close the camera back. Note: some cameras have the film chamber on the left and the spool on the right. Always follow the instruction booklet for your camera.

CHECKLIST

✓ Don't load film in bright light, to avoid film fogging (going cloudy)

✓ Make sure that the film lies flat and is lined up with the guides, and that the holes in the film fit over the teeth on the spool

✓ Close the camera back firmly and securely

UNLOADING FILM

1 When you've finished the film, either the counter won't advance or the button can't be pressed down. On this model, the film is wound back into its cassette by sliding the film rewind switch in a certain direction.

2 When the film has been rewound fully, open the back and take it out. On basic compacts and older SLRs, you have to press in a button on the bottom of the camera and then manually rewind the film back into the cassette.

3 More advanced compacts automatically rewind a film when it is finished. On many models, you can rewind a film before you've used all of it, so that you can change to another film type. Take care to leave out a little of the film leader, so that you can reload the film.

Use both hands to hold the camera as level and still as possible.

Make sure that your fingers, your hair and the camera strap aren't in front of the lens or the flash.

HOLDING YOUR CAMERA

● One of the main problems in taking photos is camera shake, which makes pictures blurred. To avoid this, hold your camera like the girl on the right.

● To help prevent camera shake, many cameras automatically select fast shutter speeds. On non-automatic cameras you need to choose an exposure of one-sixtieth of a second or faster to keep your picture shake-free.

● As you saw on page 9, there are windows on the front of a compact camera that have vital jobs to do, so don't cover them up with your fingers. Most important of all, don't cover up the lens. Remember that you can't tell whether you are covering up the lens as you look through a compact's viewfinder. This is because the view through the viewfinder is not exactly the same as if you were looking through the lens, which is what happens with an SLR.

Keep your elbows tucked into your sides. This helps to steady the camera.

Stand with your legs slightly apart, so that you feel comfortable but firmly balanced.

13

First Steps

With a few simple rules up your sleeve, you can now start to take all kinds of exciting pictures. Compact cameras take most of the effort out of photography, and guarantee good results. But it is still easy to make some basic mistakes. If you learn how to avoid these, you will get much better results right from the start. There is one popular subject that you can always have fun with – your friends.

FOCUSING

When you look at a scene, your eyes focus on the subject that is your centre of attention. This happens even if that subject is not in the centre of your field of view (the area you can see in front of you).

Cameras don't know what they're supposed to be looking at and have to be focused. This is done either manually (**free-focus**) or automatically (**auto-focus**).

Free-focus is possible with all SLR cameras, which you focus through the same lens that is used to take the picture. This means that you can be sure which part of the picture is sharp.

Most auto-focus cameras focus on the centre of a view. They use **infra-red light** to measure how far it is to the centre. A motor then adjusts the lens for focus. You can fool auto-focus cameras (see caption right) and many now have a preview option which does this.

◄ Most auto-focus cameras have a focus marker (shown here in yellow) in the middle of the viewfinder. Position this over your subject before you shoot. Here, the friend isn't quite in the centre, so he is fuzzy but the wall is sharp.

◄ This is centrally composed and sharp. You can fool an auto-focus camera. Point it at the area you want in focus. Press the button down half-way to set off the focus mechanism. Move the camera so that your friend is where you want him and press the button right down.

COMPOSITION

◄ Look at these four photographs. In the first one the photographer got everything right. Some composition mistakes were made in the other ones. Can you see what they were?

Composition is all about how you select your subjects and **frame** them (arrange them inside the picture area). Good composition creates pictures that you can use to convey all sorts of feelings and messages.

● When you look through the viewfinder on your camera you may see a frame (like the one on the focusing pictures on page 14), which shows what will be in the picture. Not all models have this.
● Make each composition as simple as possible. Concentrate on what you want to show and go in close.
● Keep your viewfinder square to the ground so that your picture doesn't tilt. Avoid making things grow out of your subject or chopping off parts of people's bodies.
● Most people try to take photos on sunny days, but be careful that your own shadow is not in the picture, unless you want it as a special effect.
● The rest is up to how you treat your subject. Share the fun and make your subject feel – and look – relaxed by talking to them.
● It may be worth having a quick rehearsal. Even professionals practise before they use up film.

CHECKLIST

✔ Be careful about what you choose to concentrate your attention on

✔ Check that nothing is growing out of heads

✔ Keep the picture level

✔ Watch out for your own shadow

✔ Try to make your subject relaxed

✔ Keep people as close as possible

LANDSCAPE OR PORTRAIT?

Some animals living in wide open spaces have excellent landscape (horizontal) vision so that they can scan the movement of other animals across the horizon. We see in a more circular way and so can enjoy both **landscape** and **portrait** (vertical) **formats**. It is easy to forget that by simply turning the camera sideways you can take portrait format pictures, which are often much more suited to your subject-matter than a landscape shape.

▲ This landscape picture draws attention to the ship and to the unusual architecture behind, while the bridge draws the eye into the centre of the picture. How do you think it compares with the portrait photo of the same subject (right)?

▲ This portrait view forms a strong visual design because it is an off-centre composition, and includes lots of sky and water.

SIMPLE SELF-PORTRAITS

If you like setting up photos *and* appearing in them too, especially with friends, it's time for a **self-portrait**. This is also a good way to learn to enjoy posing for pictures because you are in total control. Self-portraits are easy if your camera has a **self-timer**. Or try attaching a **cable release** if you have one. This is a long cable that has a remote button that you can press to take pictures.

1 Choose a good place to take your photo. This must be somewhere you can get to quickly when you've set up the camera. Avoid a place where people will be looking into the sun – this will make them squint. You also need to choose somewhere with a flat surface to rest the camera on.

2 Now place your camera securely on the flat surface (you could screw it into a small tripod like the one on page 40) and carefully compose your photo. If you are taking a picture of a group of people, remember to leave space for yourself in the composition.

3 When you're sure that you're happy with the composition, think about the exposure. Switch on the flash if it's a dull day and you want the group to stand out against the background.

Then turn on the time exposure switch. Press the shutter button half-way down to pre-focus. Then press the button all the way down and run round to join in the picture.

EXPOSURE

Getting the exposure right used to be one of the main problems for photographers. It is also the way that really expert professionals create stunning images – getting the correct exposure makes a photo come alive. Combining the right exposure with good composition and subject matter will give you great photos.

● A photo is correctly exposed when the amount of light that reaches the film records all the details of the subject accurately. The picture should capture the full range of tones, from light to dark, in your subject.

● Exposure is a combination of shutter speed and lens aperture. Compacts normally set this combination automatically, so you have little control. But on SLRs you can set a slow speed with a small aperture and get the same result as a fast speed and a wide aperture. As long as the right amount of light reaches the film, it doesn't matter.

► The photo of the boy is over-exposed. Too much light has got through, so the only detail you can see is in the shadows. ▼ The picture of the girls is under-exposed, so we can't see anything at all in the shadows.

► Correct exposures, as in this photo, give you lots of detail in every part of your picture, from the shadows to the lightest highlights. Compacts try to achieve this automatically.

Gift tags

It's a good idea to save all your photographs, even those that haven't come out as you'd hoped. Making gift tags is just one of the ways you can use spare prints creatively.

Use pictures of yourself or of a subject linked to the present you're giving, or to the person receiving the present. You can also add extra details to your tags with a felt pen.

1 Cut out your tags with a pair of scissors.

2 Fix a tie to your tags. Either tape a short length of thick sewing cotton to the back of them, or make a hole in the tag with a hole punch to thread the cotton through.

CLICK 2 Moving on

Now that you know something about cameras, film, composition, focusing and exposure, you can move on to more adventurous experiments. Try taking pictures of your friends and family in various groups, in different natural lighting conditions and in all kinds of everyday situations – from cycling in the park to a day out at the shops.

GROUP PICTURES

Here are a few pointers for good group shots.

● Try to arrange the group quickly and cheerfully – people lose patience fast, and you don't want a photo of bored, miserable faces.
● Arrange people by height. This looks more natural and means that no one will be blocked out.
● If the light is coming from one side, be careful of strong shadows falling over some of the group.
● Group pictures create a particular mood. Ask people to stand or sit in positions that express the mood you want.

▲ This is a successful shot because it shows a happy, relaxed group. But the photographer has made a couple of mistakes. One friend is in strong shadow, while another has half his face hidden from view.

▶ You might think this picture is a disaster – perhaps the button was pressed at the wrong time. But hands, legs and feet make interesting shapes that can produce unusual, dramatic shots.

LIGHTING

Light is one of the most important things about photography. When you start taking photos, concentrate on making sure you have enough light to get a good result. As you gain experience, you can work with light to make your photos even better. The photos on this page show how to take shots indoors in bright natural light. If there is very little light, you will have to use flash.

● Taking photos in natural light is known as using **available light**.
● For a well-lit indoor portrait in natural light, sit your subject by a window. This gives what is known as side light, and its harshness or softness depends on the type of daylight outside.
● Daylight will often reflect back from the walls of the room on to your subject to help light up shadowy areas. But this still won't light the subject evenly. You can either choose to concentrate instead on creating strong, side-lit effects, or use a home made reflector (see right) for a more balanced effect.

◄ Here, side light from a window has lit one side of the girl's face very strongly and thrown the other side into shadow. The photographer has positioned the girl so that some light reaches the side of the face away from the window. This gives an effect that is quite powerful, but also very natural.

◄ Holding a reflector close to the girl lights her face more evenly. Light from the window bounces off the reflector, on to the subject. You can buy reflectors from photo shops, or make your own from a sheet of card covered in shiny kitchen foil.

CHECKLIST

 Move the subject towards or away from the window to control brightness and contrast

 Tilt or turn the subject to get the amount of shadow right

✓ Take time checking through the viewfinder.

✓ Use a tripod, if you have one, to keep the camera totally steady

► This is the result of using the reflector shown above. It has produced a natural, evenly lit picture. To take a photo as good as this, you will need to spend time looking through the viewfinder and asking the friend holding the reflector to change its angle until it is just right. Your subject might also need to move slightly.

ACTION PICTURES

Many of your photos will involve action. Before you move on to more experimental action shots, there are a few simple points to think about.

● Whether you use a compact or an SLR, get plenty of experience of how camera movement, composition, exposure and focus work together.
● Try to point the camera to where the action will be before it has happened.
● Use the right exposures and focusing for the situation. Most compacts select these automatically – to set them yourself you need an SLR camera (see opposite page). But compacts still give you a variety of ways to take action shots, as the pictures on this page show.

▲ For the simplest type of action photo you point the camera at the subject and press the button. A compact can't expose fast enough to freeze the movement, so the bicycle is blurred, but the trees are sharp, which gives a feeling of action.

◄ With practice, you can take this sort of action shot. As the cyclist passes by, pan (move) your camera along with her, keeping her roughly in the middle of the viewfinder all the time. Press the button when you've got the background you want.

► In this photo, panning has been used again, but this time the flash has been switched on, even though the light was bright. This freezes the movement much more and makes the bicycle stand out dramatically against the background.

TALBOT'S TIPS

Compacts are mostly automatic, so they guarantee a good result, even when taking difficult action shots. But this means that you have less control than with an SLR camera. Here are some tips on taking action pictures with an SLR.

● Remember that different films have different speeds. For action shots, where you often need fast exposures in low light levels, choose a fast film.

● With an SLR, you can control the exposure yourself by selecting the shutter speed and the aperture. Short exposures help to freeze fast action. Long exposures provide the opportunity for amazing blurring effects. Being able to set the aperture yourself also means that you can control the depth of field.

● You can use a range of different lenses on an SLR. For example, wide angle lenses fit more into the picture and give greater depth of field. This helps with action pictures, when focusing quickly can be a problem.

▲ By selecting the shutter speed and aperture, you can create exciting action shots like this, where the background has blurred into streaks that give a feeling of speed. This photo was taken while panning with the camera. To avoid blur where you don't want it during slow exposures, either hold the camera steady or use a tripod if you have one. You may be able to fix the tripod so that it stops the camera moving up and down, but still allows horizontal panning.

▲ Here, the SLR's manual controls have been used to take an unusual action shot of a ghostly cyclist among the autumn leaves. Being able to adjust the focus control exactly has meant that the leaves in the foreground are picked out in sharp detail. A slow shutter speed was chosen to create the eerie cyclist. At very slow shutter speeds, it may be difficult to get a good result without a tripod.

OUT AND ABOUT

Everyday events, such as a shopping trip, can make excellent subjects. But taking a good picture when you are out and about in places such as crowded shops and streets can be tricky.

● In these kinds of places, you may not have enough space, or you may have too little light and too little time to compose the shot.
● If you have a zoom lens, use the widest angle setting in cramped conditions. Or zoom in through the crowd to pick out your subject.
● Switch on the flash for an evenly lit photo in awkward spots with patchy light.
● If the scene is jammed with people, try taking a chance by setting your camera controls to automatic, holding it above your head and shooting.

► In this market-place shot, the photographer got a clear view of her friends by standing on a nearby step and looking down on them. She used available light to create a soft, natural effect that looks more like a painting than a photograph. Look for scenes with splashes of bright colour – like the flowers in this photo.

◄ This shot was taken in a tight space at a cafe table. The photographer avoided everyone else and came in close on her friend drinking tea. Flash was used as there was very little light.

▲ This scene is crammed with detail. The photographer chose a low viewpoint, focusing on the antiques her friends were looking at. Don't take too long choosing your shot. This was taken a second too late and the girl's eyes are shut.

Making a birthday tree

Sally
November 28th
Loves: Dance music
Hates: Being bored

Daniel
July 14th
Loves: Football
Hates: Getting up
early

Nadine
February 9th
Loves: Ice cream
Hates: Spiders

Sean
April 6th
Loves: Swimming
Hates: Rain

Syrah
January 11th
Loves: Animals
Hates: Pink

I love:
Photography

ME
CARLY
May 3rd

I hate:
Tidying up

Craig
July 12th
Loves: Computers
Hates: Tomatoes

This idea is a variation on the traditional family tree. Use left-over photos to make a tree on any subject you like. The tree could show photos of the friends who came on your shopping trip, or on another day out, such as the funfair visit on pages 24 and 25.

1 Decide what sort of tree to make and cut a piece of cardboard to size. It might be small, so that it fits into a folder, or large, to go on a wall.

2 Cut out a simple tree shape from green paper and stick it to the card carefully, smoothing out air bubbles.

3 Choose your photos and cut them out. If you want oval shapes like the ones shown here, try cutting an oval

out of plain card, positioning it on each photo and drawing around it so that you have a cutting guide. Lay out your photos until you find an arrangement you like and then stick them down. Remember to leave enough room for text.

4 Use felt pen to draw the branches and leaves that connect the photos. Either hand-write the text, or print it out from a computer.

Telling a story ■ ■ ■ ■

Whatever you enjoy taking photos of, it is always exciting to be able to use your pictures to tell a story. Every day, photographs are used in newspapers and magazines to record incidents or to tell stories. You can do just the same, but you can select any subject you like – we chose a day at the funfair. You might want to let your photos speak for themselves, or add written captions.

It's up to you to use your camera sensibly and naturally. With practice, you will find it easier to take shots that tell a story well. A few basic rules will help.

● Use a film that is the right speed for the conditions you're likely to meet. For taking photos in low levels of light or at night where you can't use flash, choose fast film. If you're not sure what to expect, take a medium speed film or a choice of films.

● You might want to consider using an SLR camera if you are telling a detailed story where you need total control over the settings. If you are feeling ambitious, you might even use different lenses for different subjects, if you have them.

● Once you've sorted out your techniques, you need to think about your approach – what you want to show and the best way of showing it. For example, a story about a birthday party needs a different approach from a record of a sports event, or, in our example, a day-trip to the funfair.

● Don't forget to take a photo that shows the start of your story properly – like the one above of people setting off on their day out.

◄This shot was taken by putting the camera on a ledge near a funfair ride and letting it take a long exposure. The automatic flash was switched off, so that the lights on the ride lit up the scene. Including a person in the picture means that you can tell how big the cups are.

► At this funfair stall people try to knock toys off their pedestals with balls. Most compact cameras focus on what's in the middle of the frame. Here the photographer has made the stars the centre of the picture, so the emphasis is on the toys and the children are out of focus.

▼ The photographer was not sure when her friends would come out of the ghost ride, so she just pointed the camera and clicked.

▼ Take shots that capture the whole day. This photo was taken at the end of the day and shows who was there. The photographer pre-focused on the balloon to make it look sharp and sparkly and then moved the camera to include her friends and the interesting background. No flash was used.

CHECKLIST

✓ Take the right speed of film for your story location

✓ You may want to take an SLR if you have one and know how to use it

✓ Remember that you are the story-teller – take control of the situation

Making a panorama

Tell people about part of a special day out or a holiday with this spectacular presentation idea. A panorama is a long picture that shows a very wide view. You can make one up from three or more photographs taken from the same viewpoint. To create your panorama, simply stick the prints together.

CHECKLIST

✓ Find a comfortable, steady viewpoint

✓ Look around and plan your panorama carefully

✓ Overlap your pictures by at least one third

✓ Make sure you have enough film in your camera

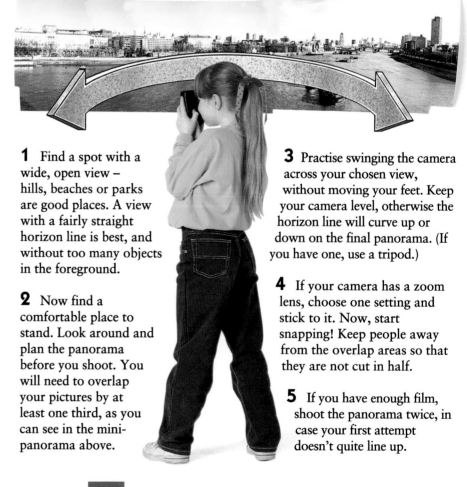

1 Find a spot with a wide, open view – hills, beaches or parks are good places. A view with a fairly straight horizon line is best, and without too many objects in the foreground.

2 Now find a comfortable place to stand. Look around and plan the panorama before you shoot. You will need to overlap your pictures by at least one third, as you can see in the mini-panorama above.

3 Practise swinging the camera across your chosen view, without moving your feet. Keep your camera level, otherwise the horizon line will curve up or down on the final panorama. (If you have one, use a tripod.)

4 If your camera has a zoom lens, choose one setting and stick to it. Now, start snapping! Keep people away from the overlap areas so that they are not cut in half.

5 If you have enough film, shoot the panorama twice, in case your first attempt doesn't quite line up.

PUTTING YOUR PANORAMA TOGETHER

1 Lay out the prints on a flat surface and look at the way the overlaps work. Arrange the pictures carefully before you glue them on to a piece of card, to make sure that you are happy with their positions. Use small pieces of sticky tape on the edges of the prints to hold them in place while you arrange them.

2 Once you are happy with your arrangement, use strong paper glue to stick the prints down one at a time, starting at one end.

3 When you have finished, and the glue has dried, trim the edges of the panorama to a neat rectangle (or cut out a more creative shape, if you are feeling adventurous). Use scissors or a ruler and a craft knife. Ask an adult to help if you are using a craft knife.

TALBOT'S TIPS

● Try a trick panorama with the same person in every shot. Take the pictures slowly, so that your model can move across to appear in each one. Keep your model away from the overlap areas.

● For a circular panorama, take shots as you move around in a complete circle. Glue your prints down so that the ends join to form a circle.

● Create unusual panoramas from shots of the same view taken on different days or with different models or objects in them.

● Use either horizontal or vertical photos. Vertical ones fit in more of the foreground. You will also get more foreground if you take two series of shots, one above the other. You will need to overlap these vertically as well as horizontally.

Holidays

Cameras are as important to the success of a holiday as sunshine, good company and enjoying yourself. Use your pictures to show your friends what you did on holiday and how much fun you had. Taking photos means that you have a lasting record, too. Video cameras are now used much more on holidays, but photographs can provide a record that is just as exciting and vivid.

ON THE BEACH

The seaside is a popular place for holidays. Beaches create their own special conditions, so keep the following points in mind.

● Try not to knock your camera about too much. Be careful near water, sand or grit. Salt water is especially damaging if it gets inside a camera. Don't get water on your lens – it will give fuzzy shots. As a last resort, keep your camera in a plastic bag, but don't let it steam up.
● A beach is the perfect place for all kinds of subjects. On a sunny day, create striking shots with wide views of sand, sea and sky. Take closer shots of people, deckchairs and beachballs, with clear, bright colour and detail. In misty weather you can take moody, mysterious pictures.
● Be careful when pointing your camera towards the sun, as this may over-expose the film. But aiming towards strong light can create dramatic silhouettes.

The photos you can see on this page have silhouettes where darker areas come out as solid black shapes. In the shot above, the photographer has bright light behind him. This reduces risk of over-exposure but means that he might get his own shadow in the picture.

◀ The strong silhouettes of the children in this photo were created by shooting into strong light.

▶ This shot was also taken into bright light, but more detail can be seen on the figures because the flash was turned on.

CAMPING

Campsites also provide plenty of subjects for exciting photography.

● The same rules of camera care apply as on beaches. Cameras are easily damaged by rain and damp conditions – so look after them. Both cameras and film can be damaged by very hot or very cold conditions. If you leave a camera in the sun, the case may become distorted. The colours in your pictures might be distorted too, if the film is damaged by heat.

● The day-to-day events of camping, such as cooking and washing up, give you all sorts of opportunities for taking photos. You can also use the shape of the tent to make great compositions.

▲ Strong light has helped to make this well-exposed, brightly coloured picture. Compacts are designed to balance highlights (brightest areas), mid-tones and shadows and give the correct exposure.

► Taking a shot from inside the tent has created an unusual composition. Using parts of figures in shadow gives interesting shapes.

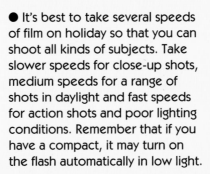

CHECKLIST

✓ Don't let your camera get damp. Keep it well away from water, grit and sand

✓ Make sure you don't leave your camera or film lying in hot sun. Never let them get really cold, either

✓ Remember that you can take great shots in all kinds of weather conditions

TALBOT'S TIPS

● It's best to take several speeds of film on holiday so that you can shoot all kinds of subjects. Take slower speeds for close-up shots, medium speeds for a range of shots in daylight and fast speeds for action shots and poor lighting conditions. Remember that if you have a compact, it may turn on the flash automatically in low light.

● If you have an SLR and different lenses you might like to take these along so that you can try out

different effects. For example, with a telephoto lens, you can take close-ups of a subject while standing some distance away.

◄ This photo was taken at a swimming pool with a disposable underwater camera. Apart from the air bubbles that tell you he is swimming in water, you could easily believe that the boy was an airborne giant floating underneath a white thundercloud. It's difficult to know whether the mysterious light above him is coming from above the pool, or from the flash.

GOING UNDER

While you are on holiday, you might want to see the effects you can get by taking pictures of people or objects in or under water. As explained on pages 28-29, you must be careful if you take a camera near water, but there are special waterproof cameras that you can use for underwater shots. Remember that you need to be a very confident swimmer before starting to take underwater photos.

CHECKLIST

 Check that it's safe to take photos in or under the water

✓ Make sure that an adult is present

✓ You can get great shots and have lots of fun with disposables – but don't expect to take perfect photos

✓ Remember that colours will be distorted in and around water

You must also make sure that there is an adult nearby.

Until recently, underwater photography was only possible if you were a professional marine photographer using special equipment. Today, there are lightweight underwater cameras that are much easier to handle. But these are still rather expensive, so have fun with the disposable underwater cameras that you can buy, which are perfect for using once in a while on holiday.

● Taking photos of people in the shallows in very clear seawater or in a swimming pool can give you interesting effects. For example, when people are partly in water, their bodies seem to bend where they enter the water, because light travels differently through water.

● Don't be surprised if the colours of shots taken in and around water seem strange. This is also because light behaves differently underwater compared with in the air.

● If you visit a marine centre or take a trip in a glass-bottomed boat on your holiday, see what effects you can get by shooting through glass.

▲ This shot was taken with an ordinary camera. It was snapped at a swimming pool, looking down into the water as the boy sat on the bottom of the pool at the shallow end. The water has distorted the boy's body in all kinds of ways – just how enormous *are* his feet! You can use the distorting effect of water to take all kinds of funny photographs of people and objects.

CLOSING IN

Close-up photography opens up another fascinating world – and it's far easier to get great results than it is with underwater photography.

● Beaches, campsites, caravan sites or hotels offer endless possibilities for close-up work that will give a different angle to your record of your holiday. Whether it's sunny or raining, you can always find something worth shooting. On the beach, try looking into little pools left exposed at low tide or take shots of shells, pebbles and seaweed. If the weather is bad, try taking close-up pictures of tickets, maps or stamps – anything that says something about your holiday.

● Close-up photography works best with slow film, which is good for picking out fine detail.

● You can take good, fairly close-up shots with most cameras, but ordinary lenses can't focus properly if you go very close. Many new cameras give you a range of lenses built into one, so that you can zoom in on subjects. They often include a macro lens too, which is perfect for very close shots. You can also buy macro lenses for SLRs.

● Remember that close-up photographs need good light to capture all the detail properly.

● You may have to take a few shots to get your close-up framed just as you want it. This is because, with a compact, you look through a viewfinder, and not through the lens used to take the picture, as with an SLR.

▲ This photo of a stretch of wet sand with sparkling, sunny highlights on the ripples would not work from a distance. Zooming in close to the sand has made the picture mysterious – you might not be at all sure what this picture shows when you first look at it.

► Seaweed and shells also look very different close up. Try taking pieces of seaweed and shells and arranging them. Then draw your fingertips across the sand to add faint patterns. Here, the light has given highlights and shadows that create a delicate feel.

Creating a holiday collage

Whether you take photos for fun, as a hobby, or for practical use at school, you will probably have plenty of leftover prints that you can use for other purposes. Using spare shots to make a collage (or a montage as it is sometimes known) is a great way to create special images that say much more than a single photograph can.

▶ To make your collage, experiment first with different arrangements of prints.

● You can see collages in lots of magazines, so look at these to find ideas. You will see that many collages mix pictures with words – try adding words or letters cut out of newspapers or magazines to yours.

TALBOT'S TIPS

● There are lots of other things that you can add to your collage. For example, if you are making a collage about a school trip to a museum, you could include your entrance ticket and part of a leaflet from the museum along with prints of the journey, your friends and the building. Or you could take close-up shots of items such as tickets and signs and include these.

● Perhaps one collage isn't enough. You might want to tell a story by creating a series of collages, each one dealing with a different aspect of a trip or event.

1 Lay the prints out roughly in the way that looks best, thinking about the space you leave between them and how they overlap.

2 Place a piece of tracing paper over your design and trace around some of the key shapes very lightly, without pressing on the prints. This will give you a guide to work from if your pictures become muddled.

3 Cut out your shapes with a pair of scissors, coat the back of them with glue, and stick them on to a piece of clean cardboard. Don't get glue on the front of the prints.

4 After you have stuck down each shape, use a clean cloth or a small roller to smooth it out lightly. This removes any air bubbles.

Here are some ideas to make your collage more interesting. Can you think of any more?

● Instead of cutting out your shapes very precisely with a pair of scissors, try tearing them. This gives a different look that can be very effective for certain types of subject.

● If you rub fine sandpaper very carefully over the back of your cut-out shapes, you can make the edges very thin. The shapes will then sit very close to each other and the joins will stand out less. This will make the collage look much more like a single picture and not a collection of separate parts.

● When you have finished the collage, you might like to retouch some parts of it, or add new details to the photos with pencils, crayons, felt pens or paints.
● Try taking a photo or colour photocopy of your collage, then sticking it on to a sheet of paper with some writing about it.

CLICK 5 Fun with flash

Modern compact cameras have a built-in flash which gives you plenty of opportunities to take photographs when the natural light is dim, or at night. You will find that your flash is perfect for taking photos of special moments at birthday parties or family get-togethers. You can also use it when you want to take shots on dark winter nights. So be creative and enjoy using your flash.

The advantage of the built-in flash on modern compacts is that it is always available for you to use, without having to carry any other equipment around.

The automatic flash on compacts is linked to a special measuring system inside the camera. This system not only checks whether flash is needed to light the scene properly, but it also sets the correct exposure for a flash shot at the same time.

● In the photograph at the top of the page, the photographer is taking a flash picture of friends as she arrives at a party. In this kind of situation, try not to stand too close to your subject. This can produce very hard shadows and over-exposed light areas, meaning that you lose a lot of detail.

● Don't forget that you can also use flash in daylight to give you extra detail in shadowy areas or simply when light levels are low.

● Be creative. For example, try night-time wildlife photography (make sure you have an adult with you).

◄ This photo of party guests outside the house in the evening would never have come out without using flash. You can see how the camera has worked out the correct exposure for the white shirts, which means that there isn't quite enough light to show the detail in the dark background. This has produced a shot full of dramatic contrast.

LIGHTING A SCENE

The automatic flash unit on a compact will give a good result in most conditions, but it is not ideal for certain situations. Make the most of compact flash by learning when it is most effective.

● Compact flash will only travel a certain distance, so it is not ideal for taking shots of large scenes. Instead, move in slightly closer and concentrate on picking out smaller areas of particular interest.
● Make sure that you don't cover up the flash unit by mistake as you are taking your pictures.
● If you have people quite close to the camera, try to avoid **red eye**.

This effect, where people's eyes look bright red, often occurs in flash shots. This is because low light levels make our eyes open up more and the flash lights up blood vessels inside the eye. Your camera may have a special red eye control to prevent this. If it hasn't, simply ask people not to look straight at the camera.

▶ You can see that there isn't enough light in this picture. The compact flash unit used to take this picture wasn't powerful enough to light the scene evenly. The best compact flash photos are taken from closer to the subject, but not very close, which would make the flash too direct and hard.

▲ This much more successful shot was also taken with compact flash. It has worked much better because the photographer moved closer to pick out a smaller group. It is also more interesting than many wider shots, where the viewer is not sure what to look at.

CHECKLIST

✓ Avoid very close-up flash photography, which gives too much contrast

✓ Make sure that your subject isn't too far away to be lit properly

✓ Try using flash to give extra light in daylight, either outdoors or in indoor shots

✓ Avoid red eye by using special controls on your camera or making sure people don't look straight into the camera

35

TALBOT'S TIPS

With an SLR, you can create all kinds of flash effects, but the equipment you need is not as easy to use and portable as a compact with automatic flash.

The flash unit fits on to the top of an SLR camera. Once you have set the controls, you can simply point and shoot, or try one of the following options.

● The flash unit can be attached to the camera by a long cable. This gives you more control over where you position the flash.

● For a soft, evenly lit effect, and no red eye, bounce the light from the flash off the ceiling by tilting the flash unit upwards. You could also try bouncing the flash off a wall. The ceiling or wall needs to be a light colour for this to work properly.

▲ This shot was taken with a flash unit mounted on the top of an SLR camera. The picture is well exposed and a large area is evenly lit.

The light created by the flash is quite harsh and the people's faces are rather shiny because the flash fired straight at them.

▲ This photo creates a different effect from the shot above because the lighting is softer and more natural. It was also taken with a flash unit mounted on the top of

the camera, but the photographer tilted the flash unit upwards so that the light was directed on to the white kitchen ceiling and bounced back over the whole scene.

SPECIAL EFFECTS

SLR flash units can be used to produce all kinds of unusual shots.

● Experiment with multiple images like the one on the right. To do this, set the shutter on a very slow speed, press the shutter button and fire off the flash several times while the shutter is open.

● For this to work, the subject you are photographing should be moving – try snapping a friend dancing and you will see different stages of the movement in one photo. In the picture on the right, movement was created by zooming the lens in and out as the photo was taken.

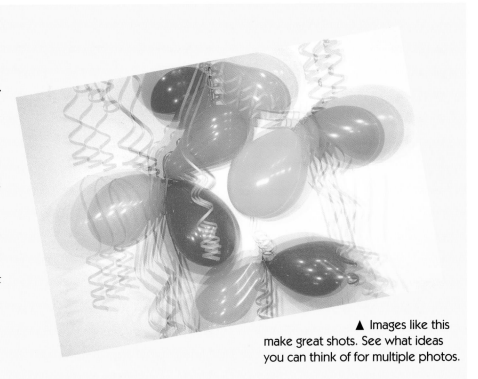

▲ Images like this make great shots. See what ideas you can think of for multiple photos.

Greetings cards

Here is another way of using your prints – to make greetings cards for your family and friends. Think carefully about your final design before you stick anything down.

1 Think about your design. What shape and size should the card be? Do you want to add things cut out of magazines or newspapers, or draw some features in yourself? Why not add speech balloons?

2 Cut and fold some card or stiff paper to form the greetings card.

3 Cut out people or objects from your prints and, perhaps, from magazines or newspapers. Arrange them on the card until you are satisfied and stick them down.

4 You could use a felt pen to draw in parts of the picture and to add some words.

Pets and animals

Pets and animals are almost as popular as subjects for photographs as family and friends. But animals aren't always easy to photograph. They behave in an independent way and rarely stay still when you want them to. You won't find it dull taking animal pictures, and it is rewarding to capture the personality of a pet, whether it is yours or a friend's.

Working with animals needs a special approach, so you may need quite a bit of practice before you feel really confident about taking photos of them. Here are some important things to keep in mind.

● If you are taking pictures of someone else's pet, it is best to try to get to know the animal over a period of time. This way, you will be able to work out the best approach. If you understand something about the animal, you can think about composition and lighting without worrying that it might do something unexpected at any time. The animal will also behave more naturally if it knows you because it will feel more relaxed.

● Take every opportunity to watch all kinds of animals carefully until you get to know how they communicate with each other.
● Always try and take natural shots of animals. Lively action photos are much more exciting than a posed picture of a pet, no matter how nice it is.

◄ This photo of a cockerel was taken with a compact camera using a macro zoom lens. It is an excellent example of good exposure in bright sunshine. In this picture, all the detail of the white feathers is perfectly sharp and vivid. If you are using an SLR camera, remember that longer exposures are needed for good close-up work.

CHECKLIST

✓ Remember that it helps if you understand animals and how they behave

✓ Aim for natural shots, not posed ones

✓ Be sensitive in the way you treat animals

✓ Don't get too close unless you know the animals well

✓ Good shots need to show both detail and movement

● Never try to pose a picture that makes an animal uncomfortable in any way.

● Take care when you get close to animals, especially those you don't know. Don't frighten them with sudden close-ups or flash exposures. Your pictures will be much more effective if they show that you have a sensitive attitude towards animals.

● Think about whether some animal photos would be more effective if you used black and white film.

● If you can, use techniques to freeze fast movement. To take close-ups, you will need more depth of field to give you vivid detail. If you have an SLR, set very small apertures to help you achieve this.

► In this photo the dog has been frozen in a lively, dramatic position. The way in which the ball it is chasing cuts into the frame of the picture creates a strong design. This is a good example of a picture that would also work well as a black and white shot.

◄ If you are photographing people with animals, position them so that one is not hiding the other, but so they look as though they are connected with each other. The best results come from being patient and waiting for your opportunity.

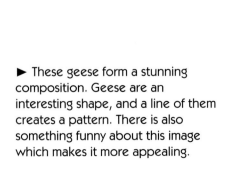

► These geese form a stunning composition. Geese are an interesting shape, and a line of them creates a pattern. There is also something funny about this image which makes it more appealing.

CLICK 7

With a little help...

Modern compact cameras have been designed to help you take good photographs in most situations, with a minimum of effort. But there are gadgets you can buy, such as camera clamps and mini tripods, which will help you to achieve even better results with your photos. You can also create a wide variety of exciting special effects by using bits and pieces found around your home.

With practice and some good ideas, you should be able to take great pictures on the most basic cameras, with no extra equipment. But you may want to take your hobby further, or find that you often have to take pictures in difficult situations. You don't have to spend a lot of money on extra bits of complicated equipment. On this page, you can see a couple of the inexpensive gadgets that you can find in any good photographic shop. On the opposite page are some suggestions for **filters** that you can make yourself. Can you think of other home-made effects you could create?

GADGETS

● You can now buy small clamps that screw into your camera and can be attached to a support, such as a door frame, table leg, or the railings in a play area, as shown at the top of the page. These clamps help you to take pictures in situations where it is difficult to hold the camera steady. Always make sure that you can see through the viewfinder easily. Clamps are also useful for self-portraits, if your camera has a self-timer.

● You can also buy mini-tripods to use for the same sorts of reasons. They can be folded up and carried in your pocket and are easier to fit into small spaces than ordinary tripods.

▲ Mini-tripods screw into the base of your camera, just like the full-sized ones. They are very light and are specially designed to be used with a compact camera – they could not take the weight of an SLR.

CHECKLIST

✓ Camera clamps allow you to place your camera in unusual, tight spots, but make sure that you can still see through the viewfinder

✓ For polarised pictures, use clean sunglasses and make sure that they almost touch the front of the lens

✓ With an SLR, check through the viewfinder while turning the sunglasses round to get the result you want

COLOUR FILTERS

Filters can be put in front of the lens of a camera to change a photo. They can improve or alter the colours in a picture, either subtly or very dramatically. They can also be used to create special effects. Professionals use filters made of glass, plastic or a clear, shiny material called acetate.

You can make your own filters from sheets of coloured acetate sold in art supplies shops. Simply cut out squares of acetate and tape them over the lens. You can create the same effect with clear, coloured sweet papers. Try taping two coloured papers over different parts of the camera lens to colour different areas of the picture.

▲ Home-made filters are simple to make. Here, a square of acetate has been taped over the lens of the camera. Both acetate and sweet papers can be attached using sticky tape or Blu-Tack.

◄ This shot was taken with a lilac and a green acetate filter butting up to each other. The join between the filters is invisible because the lens can't focus on anything that almost touches it.

▲ This moody red sky is very dark because the sweet paper used here was twisted slightly to make it denser.

POLARISING FILTER

Many professionals use **polarising filters**. They reduce the glare reflected back from shiny surfaces (such as the sea) in strong light and make colours richer. Polarising sunglasses also cut out glare. You can use them as a home-made filter by putting them in front of the lens of your camera. Make sure that they are clean first. Polarising lenses and glasses are set at a special angle, so that they cut out many of the light rays reflected off shiny surfaces.

► To use polarising sunglasses as a filter, ask a friend to hold them over the camera lens before you shoot. If you have an SLR camera, look through the viewfinder and turn the glasses round until they cut out all unwanted reflections before shooting.

CLICK 8

Creating a set

It's always fun finding unusual ways to use your photography – as you will discover if you try the project shown on these two pages. For this, all you have to do is make a simple model or set and take photographs of it that turn it into something really special. If you don't want to make a whole set, you could just shoot a small group of objects. You can choose any subject – use your imagination!

You can use your camera to create a world filled with all kinds of illusions. For example, you can make things look larger or smaller, closer or further away, lighter or darker than they really are. Depending on what else you choose to include in your shot, you can make a pebble look like a mountain or a pile of sand look like a desert.

This kind of shot can be used for a variety of projects, by sticking prints on to a piece of paper with writing next to them, or by scanning the shots with a computer and typing in text. You can see from the photo above that a great set can also be very simple. For this set the background and dinosaurs were made of painted card. There is a pile of gravel in the

foreground which completes the scene. Here are a few points to remember when you are creating your own set.

● Make sure that nothing is likely to wobble or fall over at a crucial point.
● When you are ready to start shooting, ask someone to help you – holding filters, reflectors and so on.

◄ This shot uses a mixture of simple photographic effects. If you look at the shadows, you'll see that the set was lit by bright light from the left. A fiery, red cloud spreads across the sky. This was created by taking the photo through a piece of perspex coated with an uneven covering of red felt pen marks (see top of page). If you have a compact, pre-focus on the set, not the cloud, which should be out of focus.

►Experiment with focusing to create all kinds of effects. To take a shot like this one, focus on the foreground of the set. This makes the dinosaurs stand out in a dramatic way and creates an image similar to an early Hollywood film set.

◄ This very light photo was made by overexposing the shot. This has made all the shadows in the picture disappear, which gives the image a special mood.

► More complicated lighting effects can produce dramatic shadows. This is an ambitious shot which needs extra equipment, so you'll need some help. Fit a detachable flash unit to a tripod to the right of the set (or ask someone to hold it) and switch it on. When the flash on your camera goes off as you shoot, it will set off the other flash.

Glossary

Aperture

A kind of hole inside the camera. It works with the **lens** to **focus** light on to the **film**. The aperture is like the iris in an eye, opening to let in more light in low light, and closing in bright light. On some cameras aperture size is measured in **f-stops**. A large number, such as f16, is a small aperture, and a small number, such as f2.4, is a wide one. The larger the aperture, the smaller the **depth of field**.

Auto-focus

A system that **focuses** the image automatically. A beam of invisible infra-red light bounces off the subject and comes back to the camera. As it does this, it measures how far away the subject is. A motor then adjusts the **lens** to bring the subject into **focus**.

Automatic

A fully automatic camera makes all the adjustments without you having to set any controls yourself. Most compact cameras are automatic, although some also allow you to set various controls yourself.

Available light

This is the term used to describe the amount of natural light available in a situation. Available light photography involves taking pictures in natural light in situations where you might usually need to use **flash**.

Cable release

This is a flexible lead that screws into the **shutter** release button on **SLR** cameras. Pressing a button on the end of the cable means that you can take a photograph without holding the camera. This is useful if you want to avoid **camera shake**. A long cable release is ideal for **self-portraits**.

Camera shake

This happens with long **exposures**, when it is not possible to hold the camera still during the exposure. Pictures with camera shake either look blurred, or they are in **focus**, but the image is repeated in steps across the photograph.

Depth of field

This is the area in front of and behind the subject that you have **focused** on that is also in focus. A small **aperture** gives you a greater depth of field, and a large aperture a smaller depth of field. **Wide-angle lenses** give you a greater depth of field.

DX coding

This is a pattern of silver-coloured metallic squares on the **film** cassette, and it tells some cameras what speed the film is. Not all cameras can do this, so you might have to set a control for the film speed yourself.

Exposure

The term given to the amount of light that falls on **film** when the **shutter** is open. This is controlled by both **aperture** and shutter speed: how wide open the aperture is, and how long the shutter stays open. On many cameras, exposure is controlled automatically. If you have manual controls on your camera, you can vary aperture and shutter speed in relation to each other so the same amount of light reaches the film. For example, an aperture with an **f-stop** of f16, combined with a shutter speed of $\frac{1}{30}$ second is the same as f11 at $\frac{1}{60}$ second or f22 at $\frac{1}{15}$ second.

F-stop

The size of the **aperture** is measured in f-stops. The higher the f-stop number, the smaller the size of the aperture. On many cameras, the f-stops are marked around the outside of the **lens**.

Fill-in flash

Fill-in flash can light up dark or shadowy areas of your subject in situations where you might not usually use flash. When there is very little light it can be used to brighten up the subject. In bright light, where the light is coming from behind your subject and creating a silhouette, you can use flash to light up some of the detail in the silhouette.

Film

Film – black and white, colour **negative** or colour transparency (**slide** film) – is made of flexible plastic. This has a coating that contains a silver substance and is very sensitive to light. When film is **exposed** to light, the silver coating reacts and an image is formed on the film. When the film is developed a solid image is formed. With colour film, special dyes form at certain stages in the process, to produce the final full-colour images.

Film speed

The speed of a **film** shows how quickly it reacts to light. Films are made with different speeds, to cope with different lighting conditions. The speed is measured in **ISO** (or ASA or DIN) numbers, marked on the film cassette. Slow films (ISO 25 to ISO 160) are suitable for normal daylight. Fast films are used mainly in lower light. They are also useful for fast-moving objects, when you need the shortest **exposure** time possible so that the moving image does not blur. Fast film speeds range from ISO 400 to ISO 3200. They can produce quite grainy pictures.

Filter

This is a circular or square-shaped piece of plastic or glass that fits over the camera **lens**. It is tinted so that it changes the quality or colour of the light that reaches the **film**. Certain kinds of filters can be used to cut down glare from very bright objects. Other types create special effects.

Fish-eye lens

A fish-eye **lens** has a very wide angle of view – 180°. It takes photographs that are circular, in which the subject is very distorted, with objects leaning inwards.

Flash

A sudden flash of very bright light used to give extra light in dim conditions. Flash can also be used to freeze movement. If you have manual controls on your camera, any **exposure** faster than about $\frac{1}{250}$ second should freeze most movement. Flash units are built into many compact cameras, or they can be attached to **SLR**s. On some compacts, the flash fires automatically when light levels are low. On others, you can choose to turn the flash on manually at any time, even when the light level is high enough not to require flash.

Focal length

This is the light bending power of a lens. Different lenses have different focal lengths, and each one bends light rays in a different way in order to focus a subject. Depending on the focal length, lenses make objects seem further away or closer to the camera than they really are, or give an impression of normal distance. A **standard lens** has a focal length of 50 mm. A lens with a shorter focal length is known as a **wide-angle lens**. It gives a wider angle of view than a standard lens. A **telephoto lens** gives a narrower view than a standard lens.

Focusing

This is the way in which the **lens** system in a camera moves backwards or forwards in order to make the image look sharp. Usually, you try to take a sharp picture of the part of the image that is most important, because it is not usually possible to focus on the whole scene. Most compacts use **auto-focus**, which means that the focusing is adjusted automatically. **SLR** cameras usually use **free-focus**.

You have to manually adjust the lens as you look through it to bring an area into focus. Using a wider angle lens and a small **aperture** brings more of the image into focus.

Fogging

If your pictures are very soft, grey or muddy and look flat and dull, then the **film** has probably been fogged. This happens when film is **exposed** to light by mistake, for example when the back of the camera is opened halfway through a film. With a badly-fogged film no image will come out.

Fox Talbot

William Henry Fox Talbot was an Englishman who was an early pioneer of photography. In his early photographic experiments during the 1830s, he made photograms, in which objects such as leaves and lace were pressed against glass plates coated in a light-sensitive substance. He lived at Lacock Abbey in Wiltshire, which is now a centre for photographic history.

Framing

This is the term used to describe what you choose to include in your picture and how it is composed. The two basic framing formats are **portrait**, which is vertical, and **landscape**, which is horizontal.

Free-focus

This is the method of focusing used by **SLR** cameras. You **focus** an image manually by rotating part of the **lens**.

Infra-red light
See **Auto-focus**

ISO

When you look for the **film speed** on your film cassette, it will probably have the letters ISO in front of it. These letters stand for International Standards Organization. Other letters that are also used are ASA, which stands for American Standards Association and DIN, which stands for Deutsche (German) Industrie Norm.

Landscape format

This is a horizontal picture format, produced by holding your camera in the usual position.

LED

These letters stand for light-emitting diode. This device is used for display panels on some cameras and separate flash units. The panels give you information about what is happening, such as the number of pictures you have taken.

Lens

A curved disc made of plastic or glass. Light rays from the subject are bent by the lens as they enter the camera and **focused** so that they form an image on the **film**.

Light meter

A light meter is used to record the amount of light reflected from a subject so that the correct **exposure** is made. Most cameras have a built-in light meter, although professionals use separate, hand-held ones so that they can decide very precisely how to set an exposure.

Light spectrum

Ordinary light is made up of rays of different wavelengths, each of which has a different colour. The light spectrum ranges from violet through to red. You can see this series of coloured bands in the rainbow that forms when the sun comes out after rain.

Macro lens

This type of **lens** will allow very close up (but not microscopic) photography. You can buy separate macro lenses for **SLRs**, and some compacts have a **zoom lens**, which is like having several lenses in one, including a macro lens.

Negative

A photographic image on **film**, from which **prints** are made. On a negative, areas that were dark in the original scene appear transparent, and those that were light appear dark. When the negative film is processed, this is reversed and a **positive** print is produced.

Panorama

Some camera **lenses** can photograph a very wide view, called a panorama. This is a much wider view than even normal **wide-angle lenses** can produce. You can now buy disposable panoramic cameras.

You can also create your own panorama by taking a series of photos of different sections of a scene and then sticking them together.

Polarising filter

Light usually travels out in all directions. Polarising **filters** only let light pass through in one general direction. They are put over lenses to cut out unwanted light, such as the very bright rays reflected off shiny surfaces such as the sea.

Portrait format

A vertical format photograph which is taken with the camera turned on its side.

Positive image

This is the opposite of a **negative** image. Positive **film**, also called transparency film or **slide** film, behaves differently from negative film and is often made into slides.

Print

A flat photographic image on paper, usually made from a **negative**.

Red eye

When people are staring straight at the camera and the **flash** goes off, their eyes often appear bright red in the photo. This is because the flash lights up red blood vessels behind the pupil (the dark spot in the middle of the eye). Red eye can be avoided by bouncing the flash off another surface so that it is not reflected back directly from your subject's face, by asking them not to look straight at the camera, or by turning on the lights. Some cameras have a device that helps to cut down red eye. This works by firing off a series of small flashes before the main flash goes off. The bright flashes make the pupil get smaller.

Self-portrait

Taking a self-portrait is taking a picture of yourself, which is easiest when your camera has a **self-timer shutter** switch.

Self-timer

This device delays the opening and closing of the **shutter** for several seconds after you have pressed the shutter release button. This gives you time to rush around to the front of the camera and position yourself for the **self-portrait**.

Shutter

A kind of door inside the camera, behind the **lens**. When you press the button to take a picture, the shutter opens to let light into the camera. How long it stays open affects the **exposure** – the amount of light reaching the **film**. In some cameras, the shutter and **aperture** are combined.

Single lens reflex camera (SLR)

These cameras were developed in the 1960s. With an SLR, you look at the photograph to be taken through the **lens** used to take the picture. Light from the subject travels through the lens and then hits a mirror inside the camera. The light rays bounce off the mirror and travel through a prism before they reach the **viewfinder**. The prism turns the image the right way up for viewing. The moment the **shutter** button is pushed, the mirror lifts up, so that light reaches the **film**. You can buy different lenses to fit an SLR.

Slide

A slide is made by putting a piece of **positive film** into a cardboard or plastic frame called a mount.

Standard lens

A standard **lens** usually has a **focal length** of 50 mm. Photos taken with a standard lens give an impression of normal distance. Although it makes things appear the same size as we see them, our eyes give us a wider view.

Telephoto lens

A telephoto **lens** has a long **focal length**. It acts like a telescope, making objects appear closer to the camera than they really are.

Time release

See **Self-timer**

Tripod

A device with three legs for holding a camera. Standard tripods can be adjusted to different heights and allow you to tilt the camera or move it across the scene in front of you. Tripods are useful when you want to avoid **camera shake**.

Viewfinder

The window through which you see the scene to be photographed. With an **SLR** camera, the scene you see through the viewfinder is exactly the same as the one the **lens sees**. This means that what you see is exactly what you will take in your photo. The viewfinder of a compact shows a slightly different scene from the one the lens sees.

Wide-angle lens

This is a **lens** with a much wider angle of view than a **standard lens**. This means that it fits a much wider scene into the picture than a standard lens. Wide-angle lenses also have a greater **depth of field** than a standard lens.

Zoom lens

This type of **lens** is like several different lenses in one. By changing the setting, you can take **standard**, **telephoto** or **wide-angle** shots. Some zoom lenses can be used to take **macro** pictures.

Index